MW01490314

TIGERS!

A MY INCREDIBLE WORLD PICTURE BOOK

MY INCREDIBLE WORLD

Copyright © 2023, My Incredible World

All rights reserved. This book or any portion thereof may not be reproduced or used in any manner whatsoever without the express written permission of the copyright holder.

www.myincredibleworld.com

Tigers can be found across Asia, including parts of Russia, India, China and Indonesia.

The scientific name for tigers is **Panthera Tigris**.

There is only one species of tigers, with six subspecies.

Tigers are the largest member of the cat family (called **Felidae**).

4

They can weigh up to
700 pounds (320 kg), and reach
11 feet (3.3 m) long, head to tail!

Tigers are **carnivorous**, meaning they only eat meat.

Their diet consists mainly of large mammals like deer, water buffalo and wild pigs.

Tigers are excellent hunters, with sharp teeth and retractable claws.

They are **nocturnal**, meaning they are most active at night.

Tigers have unique striped patterns on their fur.

Like our fingerprints, no two tigers have the same pattern!

Tigers are **solitary** animals, meaning they prefer to be alone.

Adult tigers only come together to mate.

While a male tiger is just called
a tiger, a female is called a **tigress**.

Baby tigers are called **cubs**.

Mother tigers usually give birth to litters of 2 to 4 cubs.

Cubs typically stay with their mother for up to 2 years.

Tigers are amazing swimmers,
reaching speeds of 18 miles
per hour (29 kph)!

They can also jump up to 16 feet (4.8 m) high, and leap up to 33 feet (10 m) across!

Tigers are endangered, with fewer than 4,000 left in the wild.

Though rare, a group of tigers
is called an **ambush** or a **streak**.

Tigers are incredible!

Made in United States
Troutdale, OR
04/02/2025

30268266R00017